I0172672

Gabrielle's Horn

Gabrielle's Horn

David Craig

RESOURCE *Publications* · Eugene, Oregon

GABRIELLE'S HORN

Copyright © 2020 David Craig. All rights reserved. Except for brief quotations
in critical publications or reviews, no part of this book may be reproduced in any
manner without prior written permission from the publisher. Write: Permissions,
Wipf and Stock Publishers, 199 W. 8th Ave., Suite 3, Eugene, OR 97401.

Resource Publications
An Imprint of Wipf and Stock Publishers
199 W. 8th Ave., Suite 3
Eugene, OR 97401

www.wipfandstock.com

PAPERBACK ISBN: 978-1-7252-8557-6
HARDCOVER ISBN: 978-1-7252-8559-0
EBOOK ISBN: 978-1-7252-8560-6

Manufactured in the U.S.A.   09/28/20

The following poems have been drawn from Gabrielle Bossis's
He and I, a book of locutions she experienced in France between the
years 1936 and 1950. Here I have concentrated on the year 1947;
the keynote for that year was "Keep going. Do good."

Thanks to Linda, as always, for all of her help.

Contents

Thank You again, Lord! You seem to go
to all lengths to fill my cup to the brim
at the end of my life, don't You?

He does appreciate crescendo, though you never get to see
much of that. Here it's a wrap-around porch, a ukulele,
the moon's large and happy face in the nearest water.

The imagination is always God's, inventing a world
because this one's got so much to spare. That's why kids
have always stayed out so late on summer nights.

It's why starlings and bats veer so close to the ground.
Echoes prove that the outside world has no end.
Mine will, of course. Dear friends as well. But the stars

will hold their courses; the sun will shine on both sides
of that street. (There was never a whole lot of difference.)
Here we get to make some choices, maybe get a few right.

Who could possibly repay? Every light that flickers
is meant to. Heaven invents our prolonged syllables,
fills the nights with the distant banter of adolescence.

Friends find things to do. Older people come outside.
Arm in arm, we walk the perpetually amazed Mr. Sniffs.
The hill's gotten a little steeper, but it's new again.

*Oh, my very little child, who has ever
lifted love to such heights!"*

Would it matter if you saw an angel? The meadow and sky
are a blanket, in blues and greens—while next door my neighbor,
saws-all in hand, has it out with two porch stumps!

Everything is so far beyond us. The days sky high
because He does, with love in rain, in dribbling leaf.
Politicians still bark, of course, make their opinions known.

But they've never slept in their clothes on the shores of the Atlantic.
So we go with love. After all, these conversations are
the fabric of heaven, though they make their plans without us.

Still, that's not a such bad thing; we can join them
later, get filled in—missing pieces intact.
Heaven is always like that, isn't it, uncovering

itself, showing you one part of your future or another,
splotching green shadows with sun? You'd think we needed
to be reminded that Jesus is here. We might keep these days

in a locket, like people used to when they wanted more
of the past. Everything's from God, like some old camouflaged
army can opener you might borrow off of His table.

You can do a great deal without seeing the fruit.

Lift high, our loss; we fill the basket with coins—
but that's as far as we get. There is no closure,
no satisfaction earned, besides a nice sunset.

On the other hand, anyone can see how good
that is! We'd just start measuring again, come up
short, without even knowing it. All that time wasted!

But back on the first hand, think of how odd we look.
If aliens were to watch us dancing like that, alone,
with no one there to complete us, what would they think,

each awkward step? They'd probably go back home—
send foreign aid, which is why we should always dress
in one sleeve, just to remind ourselves that incompleteness

is our only art: baseball sans pitcher's mound.
It's pure Chagall. None of us really sees
who we sing to. The text is so much larger than this world.

We listen for answers we can never really hear, like
his painted Jewish brides who passively infuse
the world. Contemplation is a bird with golden hands.

*Oh, My child, what power there is in My
gentleness and in the tenderness of My voice!*

Beneath banners for a sunny small-town summer fair,
kids yelling for most their worth, running the adjoining
grass—this is where we spend most of our days.

I think it's in Indiana, though we can't tell them that.
(God's softly attended moon-shaped nails tap the table.)
Things come together: our planets, the expiration dates

on the back of dairy products. This goes on all the time.
It's grace that swings open the doors: a couple
of sodbusters, into the St. John the Apocalypse bar

in Salina, Kansas. (Each of us knows the 50s
syndicated shows, the large ring lever rifle;
the world in black and white. But no! That's the muffler

shop, their old tv in the waiting room.)
The Divine voice weaves like joyful waters
through our lives, down small city streets. Each wants to matter,

but they don't, at least the way the city fathers
want them to. Our needs only begin on earth.
The mechanic meets them. His money guides us home.

You are never alone. Can you be separated from
your breathing, or from the blood that flows in
your veins, or from the very essence of your soul?

You might be called the gainfully employed as you try
to learn the language of the many. This is how we live—
often human in our concern. May we flower in the chinks

of sunny walls, our best wishes against uneven
stone. The world has us, and we'd have it no other
way. If I got the chance I'd spend my days

right here in Saint Moritz, in my folding chair
against the evening water. It's like my scalp
needs saved, pores open to meet the darkening world.

We want the more we are, the part we can never
be. This is the world breathing, the clock that owns us.
It's what's left of Calvin's heart, the approaching end.

Let me set up a second chair, try to repair the damage,
though it's always been just the two of us here. You remember
the lonely boy who could never get anything right?

You walked with him in those fields. They were Your parents
too, lonely pilgrims, not an answer in sight;
we kids, challenging the world at every turn.

My child, let our two beings be so closely united
that the you in you is no longer noticed and
all your thoughts come homing to Me.

The old woman had fallen on the sidewalk across the street;
and there it was, gift-wrapped: my chance to help!
Just before I moved, the whole of time made clear.

The unity that moves us revealed itself, showed me
that life is a lot more than gathering speed
down Cooper's ridiculous Hill in the Gloucestershire Cheese Roll.

Sure, everyone needs to find his impossible slope,
to race to the bottom, though kids there keep flying up
after falling. You know they'll bounce, but you don't want

to see it—repeatedly: broken bones, youthful
laughter. The dear old woman got caught, she said,
watching our happy mutt. Each of us races

toward age, where the falling happens much more frequently.
Our lives become a potato sack race. We, too,
will tumble, though down a more modest hill. No one

will cross that particular finish line, though the birds
will tweet our message to heaven, our first look at the place.
Purgatory will have its sun rise, its noises, too.

No two souls are alike. None other can
give Me what I expect from you.

My soul owns itself. She basks in her own sun.
She'll walk you right up your front steps, old as
you are. She used to be an orange Chevy Vega,

with a fringed blanket on the cracked back seat. Perhaps
your experience runs something like that—your soul talking
it up in the outfield. Maybe you operate a crane

eight hours, up and down. Frankly, I don't know how
you manage! I don't know much about life myself.
I dance with my wife—even when I don't.

She's the only one who knows me: the boy hesitant
to come out. Jesus is something like that, with His howdy
ears, the size of small saucers. Maybe

so He can listen—or make us feel at home.
We get so caught up in our tense little failures, don't we,
or more happily, in low clouds, the opening morning sky?

He is hope personified, isn't He? A gift until the end.
We have no idea what today will ask of us,
as it pitches its tent like Abraham, taking up some ground.

Now is the time that I veil My holiness and My justice. Do you thoroughly grasp what I am saying?

The hobo walks next to the train, heroically into
the dusty sunset. He chummed with Chaplin, Keeton,
Brother Leo, and you. You did five man bar scrums, knocked back

a few before you walked out into the bright winter light.
The earth is a flying carpet under stumbling feet.
Sometimes we felt it ruffle. This became clear

as we talked baseball or Beat writers on 13th.
It was the beer in us, the raw intent. We allowed
ourselves, finally, ourselves. (This was how we remembered

our addresses.) Courage is most available when we don't
need it. Most days our deposit goes into getting up,
feeding the dog. Our warrior wanes by afternoon.

None of this changes the call. Jesus wants adults.
Even the rear guard must soldier straight,
though surely no real battles are won from here.

Time is not in our hands. He stands right next to us.
Correction comes in its own real-time as well.
Artists fight best blindly—their battles too big.

The most beautiful gift you can give
Me is your joy in serving Me.

In the lift of trees, in bird squabbles, we try
to serve; I bounce my grandson in front of the mirror.
Jesus lives in my daughter, in what she has to learn.

It'll be just the two of them, adults down a different
aisle, one that, thankfully, belongs only to them.
And my wife, who is now almost as old as I,

we race, in a gimp, to a finish that will not altogether
please. And my Down's son. Who will care for him,
though he's more adept in the ways of the world than we?

This is where we find our joy: in serving among
the imprecisions of this place. We move through sufferings
which measure us, until death, the final cow-bell

sounds: our past then, over. It will no longer
exist—because it never completely did.
You'll be able to run your hand along a painterly wall

in heaven. Here, we try to find our place
among friends. The serving can go so many ways:
moonlit dishes—seven towels and spontaneous dancing.

Give more importance to the little things.

When you take less room, you leave more space for others.
This is how heaven gets filled. It's where we buy our tobacco,
where we trade our hides for dried peaches, some shot.

We could be ourselves generations ago, in coonskin,
riffling through the goods at Chambers General Store.
Perhaps the proprietor would be expansive, or uplift

in cursive grunts. Either way, we'd both say enough
for me to come back for round two. Life is like that:
strangers keeping track of the smallest things. Friend

or manageable foe? A possible mate, or no?
It's how we barter, in pieces. It's how we give,
as well; it's in the eyebrow. Does it start to rise?

With what urgency do we participate? Though it must be said
that even if you fail some, most people are quick enough
to forgive if you add a smile. They want to look past

their sins, to the us we all want to be: good citizens,
friends. Failures come and go. Most are small enough.
Will that be enough? The answer is always no.

*Don't speak when you should be silent. And
don't keep silence when you should speak.*

May our silence breach like a great blue. It won't
be us, after all, doing the talking. Life
is like an insistent tambourine, a many-edged chime

we can never entirely control. For example, our priest,
this Ash Wednesday, motioned for me, untrained,
to pop up out of my pew and help him cross ashes;

and then later, when I went up to receive mine, he didn't
even use the regular "Thou art dust" prayer. You know,
I just cannot figure Jesus. What is He up to?

He's a road that does nothing but widen; that is always slightly
disturbing—and which I have to admit, I like,
since there is no end here, just the noises of small animals

in the passing greenery, light mottling down through motor
scooting trees. I want my life to be a shout.
I want it to be as quiet as growth in the grass.

Grace is delivered to us in a kind of sign language.
We gesture for a Man we only partially know.
In the end, that's enough. The burden has to fit the frame.

How can you find Me if you don't hunt for Me?
                                    —A LOVE SUPREME

Trying to catch the last Coltrane: we check each saucer
and cup, note the scraping sounds; we absently
hunt the couch throw. Where is he going? Oh,

we get it, sort of: our part in this great—whatever
this is; that troll, joy, buried beneath piles
of laundry. You are someone we wear! And us? We're a scree

of answers and the good in loose design. You have,
of course, that sax: its squiggling, hurting, as it routes
our problems; pain is Your middle name, the need

you tap out with your precious fingers. And in the times between
your songs? You can be a walk along a park lake,
or the sound of chalk loudly marking my personal history.

(We teach what we know least! It's the only way
to find God!) Come with us to lunch, however you choose;
we can hunt there too! We can try to find His name.

Beggars have no say in the larger world,
mostly because they don't live here. They stand in two
places, ready to walk across and help, either way.

Your eagerness will glorify Him.

In Rossellini's movie, *The Flowers of St. Francis*, the friars
are always running. But it's not some black and white
patina that makes that happen. Its visual hope,

the thought that something has been left undone, has not
been addressed. And then there is the other side: the sin
they need to move beyond, that fallen sky.

Judgment day will be this early afternoon.
What a sight it would be for a day, to see every Christian
running! The hospitals, help houses, would be filled with urgency,

that kind of stop-and-live in their eyes' transparency.
You'd see brothers shopping apace through grocery aisles,
a calm and transcendent eagerness at Holy Mass.

More of us would look slightly disheveled, unkempt.
More of us would be barefoot, we'd sleep sounder;
as we ran, the bounding world, like a camera angle,

would fall into place—at least the parts we could know.
Our joy would be in the sorry process, our next failure.
Our joy would be in the light that fills the world.

Each soul is the object of My special love.
That is why I am so grateful to those who are
resourceful in bringing back sinners to Me.

If a door opens behind us, one has opened in front
as well. "Here comes everybody," including Joyce
who hangs in long enough to get paid: a kid's sun

pinned on the sky. Let these windy gauzy sheets
drape everyone! We'll delight in the show: foreign children
will stalk us—a hundred sunny faces pressing through.

The only sinners we can bring are the birds in our heads.
"Come in, slow ones." That's what He says because
that's the house, the summer holiday where the best of us lives.

We can never be equal to this call; we reach, then reach
again. It's the same when we talk. Jesus is what
we're selling, the answer that so overwhelms the questions

that It takes a whole new land to complete His say.
I'd learn castanets if that would help, His speech,
the quiet no ear can clearly hear. Jesus,

great God, I give you all I have: Yourself!
May I walk You. Inhere. Let my voice speak the odd-folk,
the forgotten ones who call us into other's lives.

Remember that nothing happens without
My permission, and be very serene.

No stone turns, no water finds its way down these ancient
steps without Him. There are only fine rice fields,
so many new black-haired friends who make each morning;

the cities they build. You can't speak that language (or the others);
an opened hand is all one needs. A smile
can go a long way as you imitate the sounds.

What matters is the want that always breaks through. This is how
everything happens. First there's nothing, and then, bang:
a universe is, and some person in front of you turns,

friendly in the grocery line A whole world opens.
You're a stranger—or, rather, still one, fumbling through each
new situation. This is His land. And you are grateful

to be a perpetual newbie. It makes you happy for clouds.
Every new friend reveals part of His ploy:
He wants to take us alive again, to make us

into something entirely new. And who could blame Him?
Creation demands as much. Even the grasses
in heaven—trying to figure out what happens next.

*Oh, My little girl, have faith in the great
things that you can do with Us.*

Greatness comes on a high horse—changes you.
When greatness clatters, you get out of his cobble way.
(You're not the only guy who can lift a pen.)

Greatness doesn't consult you. He comes with a retinue,
sets up shop to show you who you can be. Once inside
your house, he turns it into something else. He sits

in a new living room chair, His movements disturb the fish.
We sit at His feet, wait for what He has to say.
(Sometimes His mother is there, calmly serving.)

He can make you a little anxious, but that is the price
you pay for your sins. (You just keep changing your clothes.)
Then He turns to you, provides you with the details.

He lets you know that you've been born for this,
that His favor is yours. He stands and leads you into
your dining room. You almost begin to feel

at home. His laughter contains heaven, His reach
has an alien ease. Then He rises, standing, is somehow
the room as well. You want Him—that kind of self.

Offer your death to Me now with complete
detachment, ready even for heroism.

No wind blows in those trees. Your life has come down
to this: the last brackish waters, darkness. After all,
it isn't as if you've earned anything better.

Let it count you among the unworthy. Take it on a march,
in happy cuffs. What do we have but what
we've done, a life made up of stop-gap plans,

half-appeals? Still, He is what He is, no matter
how we finish, and we're happy with that as we get pushed
along by the butt end of rifles. Birds may not

sing this night. They wouldn't help if they did. We can hear
the metal bracelets, catch some of this rising shoe dust.
We have to cough as we walk. This is not heroism.

This is what's left of your sorry departing life.
Someone else decides. He's worthy no matter where
He goes with this. (You've always known about your betters.)

Will doors appear, creak open with morning? Will loose cannons
aright? You've never had a say. So you drop your head.
Mercy will choose Its will—from a different place.

You see how awkward I am at asking? Your
freedom often prevents Me from saying
what I should like to say to you.

The twisted, bent tree wants to walk straight. His half-covered
eye, under a sag of wood, would align with the other;
his creaky limbs would cohere. It's surer this way:

the trudge, and though he knows that's a good, he also
knows that he will inch nowhere soon. The cringe
in his stiffer left leg is petition. His lane is for the slow.

Others, angry, pass by. Let us beg at the cellular
level. Lord, let Your voice be his answer, his smooth path.
And though that will not change his plight, his stride,

such as it is, or the glory he can give You,
it will be enough. Thankfully, he can't fool himself
on this road. No one will flatter him, stop, inquire—

it's a blessing every time that never happens!
His palms are fiber, his feet have no feel for asphalt,
for the paint on cement. Well, he'll let that be.

He should've brought a water-skin. Low clouds, distant,
offer Himavant, birds in his limbs. Jesus is why
bark travels, why he breaks a ridge with every single step.

Reticence suggests regret.

Consider it a bit of a stutter, Lord, the man
with too much to say. He wants to find the right words,
but the assembly line is union. Generosity begins,

apparently, at time and a half. He needs the help.
Community matters when you wear these long white robes,
Noah-like beards. I should have been an apostle,

one of the ones whose name I can't quite remember.
That way, I could enjoy the graces without the scrutiny—
though that's a dodge. I confess, I try to hide.

My cowardliness is at the root of this. I am slow
because I lack faith. Truth always comes too late,
which is, no surprise, perfect timing. Even

when I'm on the right track I'm always too slow
coming out of the gate, fussing and complaining. I'm the man
who says no, then repents, drags his body along

like a supine child. (They're never pleasant company,
these two.) Perhaps if every day were Sunday,
I could dress them up, take them for a drive in the country.

I should like you to acquire the habit of seeing
Me in everyone, in the little daily incidents too.

Blood changes the damp fall leaves; like a thousand Holy Face
medals, a bright and shiny-tinged pour of coins,
it parts the clouds. Saints have set up shop here.

And who could take these deaths, all the noise in this world,
from us? His blood is the shadowed stream we walk next to;
His labored breathing is the autumn air, red trees.

The soil fittingly breaks up the composition of leaves.
That's why the cross, the thorns, will be there in heaven
(and why we needn't fear a second fall).

Anywhere you stand on this trail, blood courses through
our genealogies, our veins. Its alleluia sings
the shucked corn. It's sweet to be where He was;

to know a little of His bloody hands, his feet.
Each drips with what we know of this human life.
Death and blood will make us like Jesus, transient,

but sure. We mark our God's way through the seasons.
This water is alive because blood will not be moved.
The smallest bark of floating leaves cries out.

To see Me everywhere would be to think of your
Savior always. Make an effort to do this as you
commemorate the last fortnight of my life.

In some small way we do this when we walk barefoot
into a two o'clock kitchen, not knowing what will be
demanded of us, but knowing, there, that someday

it will be our deaths. You are there, too, when we walk
into the living room to see a movie. We know
it's the end, and not the popcorn, that will define us.

Later, birds will sing the morning in. Our hearts
will ache in the beauty that always seems to follow.
We'll close the wooden cupboards, those doors to the dead.

We're happy to incite riot in the backyard as we
cut grass. Life prickles as I sweat, but I'm not taking
these limitations lying down. I must extend God's will,

into all of my life. What else do we have to give
but our will and the next moment? My crosses are seldom
huge, but I want to carry the garbage can

like it's my last lift on earth. (I will fail at this,
too.) My lawn shears, cast aside next to the raspberries;
our minor burdens are all that we can bear.

Just as wrong desires are the source of all evil,
so good desires are the source of all good.

Often it's like a prayer, this prayer, hands folded
or not, either at one station or at all of them.
To the good—or not, each soul attends and waits

upon that answer. Life is so tenuous. No flower
knows what it is. No plant lives where it
can be, finally, happy. And that is why

we must know the sorrow of our unholy family,
try to draw near Him, though we cannot feel His tread.
Our motives are beyond us. They squint like the stars or sequins.

We are one of those who desire the desire for good.
Each friend is twice removed, and so no friend
at all. We look for heaven's breadcrumbs—must see

we can't. We are the trees behind the wind,
something given. We mirror a passage: maples
moving without wisdom to say where, which is why

He's as subtle as He is, using everything,
even sin to craft our way home. How often we walk
between, saying yes, living somewhere else.

The grace for this Easter: in the future
you will live by Me and in Me alone.

Suffering is the handmaid of the Lord, a prophetic greenery.
The sun moves there, in a new incorporeal course.
The Word, the earth itself, will have finally been spoken!

The saints will have come to rest awhile on this grass,
under this changing sky; before His victory
lap—the settling in of heaven's doorstep.

What will He think then? The hard work has been done.
Now it's all loose ends, a bold tidying up.
A thousand brooms, a job for each member of the family.

We'll be able to grab a smoke too, if we need it. A solitude
bequeathed. The sun rises again, a pot is on the boil.
Every moment, we tell ourselves, is a call to clap

our hands—a chance to lift our couch feet. The rest
is coming. How else could it end? We will rise up again,
my friend, and unselfconsciously; we will take back

the whole of this physical world. We will learn how to churn
butter, bake bread. I will call on you, and you
will answer as you have, even before you knew.

*Of course, My poor little girl, I love the nothing
that you are so much that if you give Me
permission, I take up all the room in you.*

It was a nice, soft rain, high spare leaves and all
the early summer yakking anyone could use.
We were younger then, and much smarter this time.

We might've gotten the whole hippy thing right, our hair
would gather; we could play an acoustic guitar. Girls
of every kind would like us for no apparent reason.

Your whole life could be like that, outside, in northern
California. There'd be Napa white, jazzy places to go to
when the Pacific sun goes down. Children would come—

and our better have, named after parents and saints.
Nothing could have gone any finer. They still sit
with me and mom in front of the tv. We binge

on sci-fi, talk alternative characters. Who could've
prepared for something like this: the small breath that always
comes in and changes us, until the night settles down?

We can repay nothing. There's a sweetness beyond the telling.
St. Francis knew Him in physical nails, the points
which caught in dirt. We're not up to that as yet.

*You to whom I confide these secrets in the silence
of your heart, be this friend who believes without
seeing, and outreach yourself with the sure
knowledge that you have never done too much.*

Jesus must always see what He completes,
even in heaven. That happens in town as well:
spring has been so slow to fill the year,

though enough to make a small difference: the startling
green, where Elijah, the little boy next door,
lies on three swing seats, hammock-style. Jesus

calls. That's the secret. Home sloshes in wet boots—
after school, in birds that sing around them as they make
their way back to mom. What could we possibly give back?

The ceramic noises of supper being prepared?
We proceed with what passes for our re-given lives.
We're pleased to try again, though we know that what

we'll end up with will be nobody's idea of home.
Still, these praises must finish what we can only start.
In heaven our houses, our lives, will finish their revisions.

It's the Builder's joy to behold. (We're happy to fetch
more wood.) I imagine the weather there will be sunny.
The morning stars will shine, through a cup of pale blue.

To burn would not be enough. You must be
consumed. I mean you must burn right out.

Who wouldn't want it so, the last performance
on a stage in Toledo, Ohio, burning "right out"
in front of audience noises, seven people?

They each have a name, the same cold weather outside,
perhaps a few have no one to greet them when
they get in their door. Maybe a cat, the hum

of the refrigerator. The rain still beats steadily
on their window panes; the plain kitchen table offers
a place to reflect on what it is they've just seen.

What does it mean to be human? Where's the place
for love? They could put on a Noh mask right there
in that light. They could remember when they fit in.

You will meet that person on a downtown bus today.
He will be carrying one bag of groceries. He'll look more
or less like the others. No one will know that he's not

from here. This is how you've spent your days. This is why
you give up your seat so often to older folks:
because you're an alien. There's too much to try and understand.

Tonight when you went to your open window to
look at the splendid sky strewn with stars whose
light glinted among the flowering cherry trees, you
listened to the nightingale of the island and you
felt the joy of having so powerful a bridegroom.

Firstly, I'd like an open window in France,
in 1947; and then Jesus as a confrère
to wile away time—under a rush of cherry blossoms.

Horrible Fords had not yet been invented,
nor Chef Boyardee. Americans did not yet know
they'd won the war. There was nothing but spring in the air.

This is how things get in Weirton. You turn over in bed,
confronted by your dog's dull claws. Old joy happens
when you let children into the house. They run around

screeching, for decades, and then it's the next round:
a grandbaby—and you can't wait to see who he'll
become. (There is no end to this goodness, intruding.)

And You, yes You, always there, though You do not speak,
casting Your bread on gentle waters. You call
when it pleases You, too much of France in Your head.

All that romantic stuff, You gave rise to it:
happy endings, those nicely marching tin soldiers.
I'd like French quilts on my bed, to speak so to my wife.

You don't have enough trust. Who will give Me
this look of abandonment that I'm waiting for?

I think of Francis, naked, dying on the ground:
cold earth room; he wanted to leave, to feel
his body slip away, like a shelf of wet sand.

When he spoke, no one could hear much of what he said.
God, again, not answering, outside of the October trees,
His pain, offering the only light the man needed.

What had started as knighthood had become a wandering swayback
which could only circle itself. Any route was the same.
It was death's dance: the earth as it knows itself.

The scenario would've seemed absurd to anyone else,
with no one—except the brothers—to clean up His mess.
He'd asked them to sing him penitential psalms.

They were still a voice that too few heard: the last door
to open. He could only present who he was, an outsider,
a man without a route, a sore. And when he walked

into heaven, everyone saw him, as if for the first time.
(They would call him by a thousand names.) He waited
through one last gathered, momentary, playful silence.

Reach the degree of intimacy that I've
desired for you. Make the breakthrough.
Enter into the realm undreamed of.

We always start with nothing. And that's just the beginning.
Life diminishes from there until our only recompense
is the night sky: starry whispers and the scars on the moon.

This is what I know about intimacy: Jesus lives here.
He writes His name on my four walls. He grows
in the grass between slabs of sidewalk. My own biological

brothers know Him though they never speak His name.
He is the bright sigh who makes this place; He's a me
I cannot reach. May He dance my final room,

those frayed curtains. I want Him to open what opens,
to invite the dogs to come out from underneath my Appalachian
porch. I want Him to pray me alive. May my hands

finally bridge the waters in prayer, may they ferry
my sorry behind to heaven, bring my nephews
as well: those loveable snide low-riders, West Siders,

those whose charity has come before the fall.
I want the outsiders to know change, see town-Jesus shine.
What would the night sky feel like after that!

Give me your trials unstintingly. I may be in need of
them to save a sinner, don't you think?
                                    —for my mother

We'd like to give what we've already overcome, but that
would make us a fiction. We're poor, live closer to my mother's
childhood: drop seat-ed nights, near the wood burner.

Jesus, You didn't come as intellectual fodder.
You came for the smallest, for us and our family's children.
You came into small Ohio Depression towns,

made them, one by one, Your own. Part of us still asks
to hold fast to those three room houses, where my mom
slept in the kitchen. But the truth is, mostly we wait,

in a modern, more sordid world—no cornmeal spread
on cleared floors for radio dancing. Our burden
today is arrogance. Grandpa Henry's Jew's harp might've helped,

but he died at forty. Rheumatic fever, for you,
was a second baptism; your husband bringing back
bruising from the war. Then his polio, eight small children,

curtain clothes. Our trials arc from the old country,
beyond that. We carry our pack through an opened door,
take family with us, the cross's merciful more.

*And may the moments that remain for you be nothing
but goodness and tenderness—the gift of yourself.*
                                    —for my older sisters

My older sisters got it wrong. I am God's gift:
a softened and cooked sweet potato, a brother
who can give, despite himself, his share of recess.

I don't want to mis-number the things I have to give.
The world wouldn't be the same without my little light.
And, really, how can we love others without a patch

of grass for our own recline. Didn't He come
for each of us? Aren't the holes in His hands proof enough?
Hasn't His attention already allowed for some ease?

Jesus, bless my sisters, senior ladies now,
each having retired to warmer confederate climes.
It's not easy to love the familial rack that's stretched us.

But how else could this process ever have worked?
The good clunks along in us—like a first rate little
brother, dressed in levi's and tees: a blue day.

You probably would have recognized him through time, but he
didn't want to give himself away. Even now,
he might be a flower—casting glances in a wood.

Be full of indulgence and compassion for everyone.

How else can heaven be heard, but on West 88th,
where the world's commerce is still being worked out? In friends
who do not know that yet. The world routes itself:

in cargo ships finding the harbor, too much
of the dock. There are yells, harangues, even before
the plank extends; each side, though maddened, is filled

with expectation. Who could count the booty, the portside
domestic scene? There are balance books, lives
that have taken far too many wayward turns.

Still, everyone is filled with this day, one that hasn't really
even started yet. And they'd better be because time
has its cargo too! The people each deck hand will meet,

the goods to be exchanged, some of it visible!
Too much to keep track of, the dynamics are well beyond us,
so who can speak of just deserts? The game

has not been played out, will never be as long
as we take breath. The squeak of the gangplank, the slosh
of narrow water, these tell us what we need to know.

Abandon yourself to the strokes of the chisel; everything is for your good.

The roughness pleases, the sweat, the flying chips,
Michelangelo swirling like the plague on ladders,
boxes, talking to stone; then the sun outside.

Breaks were never that, just time to adjust
his conversation with the rock, each side wrestling,
pushing. The thing had to rise into its singular shape.

He knew the joy that God takes in every day.
The physical world required that: adjustment, movement.
Sometimes he felt the rock was like the moving sea.

It was all only the beginning as chips soon became
thinnest shavings, a polish. Then he was out the door,
to the baths or to wine, a warm dinner outside.

The lightning of God had, thankfully, struck again.
(That was His doing.) Our hero was thankful he had
a body. He was thankful for the sand in windy streets.

Life was in the next project: God's hand again,
making his beating heart. Stone did that best.
He and God met there, in muscles' deepest memory.

I have called you to union. . . . There is
still time. You will console Me and you will
make amends for yourself; you will give
Me, as it were, a taste for forgiveness.

This is how the egg bests the chicken: a whole culture
in a quiche. Great nations. Add five eggs and you get
Versailles, the plains Indians. My old neighborhood

reached its crescendo one Saturday night. I wasn't there,
but that's beside the point. Jesus was, and that
was the thing that called us. The oneness we've sought has always

had its voices; it's how it laps itself. Old friends
become old again. Forgiveness peaks above bar stools.
And back in my kitchen, the happy lilt—and cellophane!

The tiny windows will make you smile. You go
to a ball game on Wednesday, but the big picture will be
too much, so you'll study the pitcher, his body language.

It's like that with our sins; we're more deeply implicated
than we can imagine. A thorough study won't set them
right. They twizzle with the martini olive, sit at home.

Forget them, they don't matter because your hands will be His
as you try to make amends. His mom will encourage:
"There's still time. Give more of yourself—the closer you get."

And when you hold a sweet joy to your heart, welcome
Me in it.

> *—after a "Be like Ed" dream*[1]

Ed Ross shapes the world. He pushes boundaries,
demands a new name for everything. He makes rooms
for horses, for the canter. You can take up a new occupation.

Ed is what makes your hair grow. You cannot escape him.
This is his show. He comes home in the evening when the world
is quiet. He chirps, disguised as crickets, high grass.

He speaks your name when you pour out a glass of milk.
He's on the sports site, inviting you the rest
of the way home. (He's in the snort of a bulldozer.)

Little kids know this best, ramming the plastic thing
over a hill pushing the dirt away.
Children everywhere wear and make the dirt holy!

This is how we live, a yes to Yes, on a dutiful
construction site. (You've always wanted a yellow hat.
And plans! Rolls of them, under your white shirt arm.)

Ed owns us, rents little boats at the Wheeling park.
And though you feel ridiculous, your feet, paddling,
you know this place is as good as anywhere else.

*If people contemplated My creation more often than the
works of man, how this would draw them nearer to Me.*
       —Northern panhandle, WV

The mildewed houses deep in the sticks: they tend
to be a bit beat. They might have a few more cars,
decorations, wood poorly stacked alongside the house.

If the home is in deeper, there might be a chicken coup,
a smaller out-building or two, some equipment, rusted,
unrecognizable to all but the locally skilled.

Man's scene always roughly complements nature's,
failing at every turn. Monied versions are even
less true; they mulch the bushes in white gravel.

March helps. Though bare trees, at first, don't seem like hope,
they are apt metaphor: our skin, unmasked. And then
the next phase: nature expands, crocuses bloom;

cloaked in a modest majesty, they stand against
hard winds and hail. This reminds us that beauty fades.
Country songs from passing pick-ups help,

twang the age-old theme: what we're best at is loss.
But then more—June! You can stop, open a car window,
hear the small stream. God dapples, offers Himself.

If you offered Me your joys and your moments of
recreation, I would send you few trials because it is
only your union with Me that I am seeking, and as
a rule you come to Me only when you are unhappy.
Then come—oh, come always.
                    —shooting baskets with Jude

Barefoot, late, in the kitchen, the ages of man
rummage through the cupboards. My needs are vague, but since
I'm just passing through, I check the food supply.

I am looking for God again—try to focus that
as we take to the backwoods basketball court. God
is in the iron basket, the surrounding trees.

He braces the day with a late spring wind, as we bounce
the massively over-inflated ball toward the hoop,
playing the ricochets. God's in that, as well, though we

never know what He's up to. We work our bodies,
just to keep them in the physical loop. (Franz Mesmer
spins to his left on animal energy! His cross-over's

been magnetically charged with the workings of the Holy Spirit.)
The earth sings out its awkward praises of God.
Neither me nor my son are ever finished! This is why

there's time left on the playground clock as we work
our crazy angles, the unforgiving caroms and the distance—
none of it made to get us past this happy moment.

It's not the lips that should pray, My little girl;
your heart should look at Me and speak to Me.

Lips come in, mid-stream—they move with the trees.
Either way, we pick up the prayers we've put down,
maybe motivated by a nice day. They change us, no matter

our insistent sin. God speaks, and then He listens.
(It really comes down to the same thing in the end.)
The trick for us is to shut up. We beg You for humility,

for that camping place beneath the stars, for my wife,
walking down the stairs, filled with her concerns.
Hopefully, we stay in the background, our dog in playful,

sprinting mode. Neither approach keeps God on a track:
praying or being prayed, we shake like leaves,
or answers, almost forthcoming. This is why we keep beads.

If we attend, they too might be invested with heart.
We want to be our only prayer. Jesus,
take my pomp. Your broken heart would fit mine

into the cold bright bag of heaven, where Mercy insists
on Its saving darkness. There will be days to spend there,
nights to sit for others, holding no hand.

When you give Me your confidence—it's then that
I enrich you. Oh, this glorious exchange where
the one who receives the least is the happiest![2]

Jesus will not be outdone. He's like that early
morning when a rabbit broke across the frosted yard.
It made me feel like maybe Keats could be happy.

Happy again. And what will it be like to meet him,
or Shelley? "Yes, I was poor, Percy, I admit it.
No crest to bear my family name either. Still,

we both got to see the sun ball up—though I never
rode a circus elephant!" What matters to you, matters
to me, my brother. Let me walk along your springs

with you, your Italian cities. God must feel
like this. So many new stories to hear. We roll
them out: each new, each time. He delights in the near

echoes, can remember what it took to get us there.
Who could contain His joy? Who could stop our boyish
stomping? We and God, finally friends—though Jesus

has gotten too little from us: a remembered glance,
a rite of spring. When summer finally comes,
He expands; we feel leafy breezes, face and faces.

Remain very little, close to your mighty One.
                                    —Alsace-Lorraine

There's more room for everyone there. No one's reach
exceeds his grasp. That is where the Spirit always dwells,
in a little German-French house! Humility, after all,

has only one face—and it's never yours. (Five thousand
square miles can call it home.) Jesus upsets
one apple-cart, and then the next. But this

is how cobbled roads turn for everyone—away.
So some neglect is unavoidable; age shows through;
think of the cities: Alsace-Lorraine! They need work,

yes, but they offer a lasting charm. The peasants,
the guildsmen in bell-sleeved blouses know this world.
Birds can fly off, but you just have to let them go.

Oh, the fields might sorrow for a time, but that passes.
The dew comes and everything decides at once to start over.
Our tools and projects are limited, but passers, unsolicited,

are kind enough to pause, perhaps give advice.
(Every man becomes a carpenter!) You'll offer each drink,
enjoy the chance to break, the good conversation.

What I give surpasses your poor little means
and awakens new feelings in you—feelings you
thought to be beyond your power to experience.

I want angels, too, sighing in exposed rafters—
though I have no idea what they would talk about:
"Junior's hopped the fence again. . . . What's for lunch?"

My sins cover me like a minor leprosy, though Jesus
stands patient—with towel and soapy water. He's expert
when it comes to ineptitude, the rights of man.

"Don't forget behind your ears," as my mother would say.
You quietly obey. (There's a first, they say, for everything!)
You sit, quite clean, on a fallen log out back

by the pit. Our lot is true, if hard to maintain.
The stars come out, full of promise—each named!
But we've been made new so many times.

What does one do with a diminished thing, Mr. Frost?
Wait until our bones mend their crooked ways?
Invent a Rumpelstiltskin to save our magical day?

What can we be except who we are? Lord, give me
my brokenness, the rocks in my ruin. Flags flap so freely
there. It's almost like we're already home.

*The unexplored domain amazes you and proves that
it is I Myself who act in your attentive and docile soul.
                                    —during the quarantine*

Docile artists! One wonders how that gets done!
Though each poem certainly is an "unexplored domain,"
a field, untilled: hope's unuttered syllable—

a prayer. Like each day, it waits for Jesus to fill it
with fresh, chilled blackberries: one of those slatted
wooden boxes, smaller containers within.

Or we could start with a single berry, a juicy
explosion, nearly spherical, each black drupelet—
on the vine! The tiny alleluia each one is.

A grown daughter and a son would work just as well.
You weep knowing that one day they will not be seated
next to you, binging sci-fi during a quarantine.

There'll be no banter, revealing their hearts and needs;
a healthy separation that death will make complete.
(What you wouldn't do to save them from an ounce of pain!)

You'll never be a saint like Faustina, the gods in our
panoply. What we have is scratched by a faulty pen.
May it do all the things that we, unsettled, cannot.

Do you think of yourself as one not yet born? Your real
birth is your entrance into the other life. Prepare for it.

May we feel poverty's dark roots grow, push
with them against the soil—the small noises
they make. Worms must be privy to that silent cacophony.

Birds will attend, adjust their heads, calculations.
Our lives are a birth pang, the sigh of God, the shape
of an act as we give ourselves to process. We can't

escape the pain as we stretch beyond cracking skin,
beyond a world which would have it another way.
It's always silent here, good but confining. We're not finished,

growing into and out of ourselves. Others, no doubt,
do the same. It's what binds us together. It's not our address,
the one we don't share with our families. Lord, You own us,

teach us to forget the ancient battle. We can only
follow the spirit that needs release, can only
imagine the final creak that will finish us, the Word

that will turn us into You. You know this dark,
its John of the Cross nights, what it's going to take.
So we'll keep preparing—what is against what isn't.

*These give Me to others unawares, for the Spirit
possesses them and expresses Himself through them.
—for the virtuous pagans[3]*

We all enter heaven wearing someone else's shoes.
We'll be judged on how badly they fit. Buy big shirts!
(Most of our yeses come from somewhere else.)

That is why clock towers sound the same time—
because Heaven opens every day at exactly three o'clock.
Jesus is the risen generosity that sustains us all.

He wrote his first religion into our hearts.
He was alone on that pre-mountain, and being a family
man, He made us from sacramental soil.

St. Anthony of the Desert called God's first book "earth"—
where everyone assents by just walking around the joint.
And when we try to help, it doesn't even matter

if we miss the mark because the effort is the goal.
(We've opened the final door.) The Spirit rises
with the sun, breathes His commands to the flowering highlands,

everyone on the same page, whatever the number.
Our voices fill in the spaces in heaven's canticle,
make it new. Change becomes us—though it hardly arrives.

(Lourdes.) Break free of yourself. Take note as to
whether even here, you are acting for Me or for you.

I want a sandaled walk to the forum, our robes
shaking out, cool in the evening; we might come to hear
Plato, where everyone is almost quietly praying—

like sheaves or the inundations in a field of wheat.
Quiet is welcome, measures us here among the rock,
grotto waters. So many in need, in Masses

underground. An army of wheelchairs armed against
the self. Holy places are so sane! Gothic
cathedrals, an isolated bench in a park. These things

reveal us. The name might be ours, or one of our children's.
It's the place of right living, where the sky is like coolest
water. Didn't I know you when we first met!

Wasn't your voice part of mine? We could be quiet
there because words would not have helped us. Still,
we cannot break loose from our fallen sense of self.

The crippled can't walk, and seeing that is their
first miracle. We can only offer what remains of us,
crutches beside us as we shade our candle, sing our hymns.

*Ask My mother for the grace to live like her, in our
company which is more real than all the visible world.*[4]

You can be yourself there, talk with Robert Bly
under a box elder tree; you can drink the darkness
that rusted farm machinery affords. And why

wouldn't you? You've always liked those Minnesota places,
though you've never been. You'd like to think there's a plane,
small prop, older than you'd ordinarily be comfortable with,

puttering in the background. There are so many places
that own you, or could. That's what timelessness is for:
your family, though they're nowhere around at present. You'll carry

them to them if you get it right. Just now it's
the northern plains, some stars and moonshine. St. Francis
is there, looking for a moment into the crackling fire.

You can unburden with him as sparks rise. In every
case there's more to discuss; not because you're alien,
but because you're not. There will always be the next question.

Heaven was made for that. You'd think Mary's house
was far away, but you're there, have been so, each time
you've sent breath against the night sky, or sat on a see-saw.

I'll give you My love and My patience for your
neighbor; you will have a clearer understanding of
the fact that he is I, and you will go to him for love
of Me, very simply, always with the thought that
you are less worthy, like the least among all souls.

This china shop widens for bulls. They trot up and down
the crystal aisles without a care in the world.
A snort is what one gives. Why do you need more?

My neighbor is always bearing gifts. Each meeting is a surprise,
like a rough-hewn wooden rail fence. I never know where
the talk will go, but it will probably include his kids

or his job, for which I'm grateful. Who has any answers
here? We offer our lives, without any sense
of what we can give. We could be a newspaper, or a pear.

Love is our gamble. We'll search around inside,
making racket as we talk, maybe finding something rusted.
We bring it out in the sun—even as we mind

the conversation's arc. Jesus, take this. Give us
the humility to persevere right until the last word.
(And then it's, "How did I do? . . . Not well I fear.")

Every part of our life is like the rest of it.
We're little entertainers, serving up soup in a line
for a people who save us. We try to remember each name.

*What immeasurable harm can be done by
a bitter word! I alone see the extent of it. So
limit your influence to the most exquisite
gentleness and you will obtain more.*

Maybe if I paid more attention, I could move past
these nagging memories. We repent again when the guile
it took to unnecessarily hurt another reveals

itself. Hatred, in layers. It's a mistake to fool
ourselves. This is always the first step. The last is theirs,
His. And here you are, again, on a hill of sorts,

raking leaves, free as a suburban September.
Two cars in the garage. But the pressure is there—improve
or die. This is why He takes you to the park, feeds birds.

The next person I meet will decide my fate.
Taking my daughter out to lunch will ring through eternity.
We didn't invent this place, though we do ourselves:

the ratty chair pulled out with some grace, picking up
her curlers, comb, in the bathroom. (May they bring her home.)
The others: those I hatefully asked to bear the weight

of my sins. That was my gift to them. I could hang
my head for eternity. It would not help me stand.
This is why older people struggle to kneel. They remember.

You remember how an angel came to stir up
the pool for the healing of the sick? No one
knew when this would happen. That's the
way the Spirit comes. So listen for Him.

The Spirit hides. Who knows what makes us ready?
A movement of our crossed bare feet? A rip in the calendar?
We never know. He just chooses to break through,

and our notions get some air. This must happen often
as we're always ready to settle, sediment in our minds.
But the good man is always waiting for completion,

even when it comes. Everyone has so much
to learn, owns no time to make that happen.
He who made us, made these days which add to our number,

even as they push us toward the pit. May we fall in the only
line there really is: obedience. Lord, help me
to be grateful for my weakness. Praise always starts from some other

place. We pick up a strain that has gone on long
before us: that angel, that pool. It's heaven's ache.
We get to the water, a nobler etch of eddy—

too late. Paying attention is all we can ever
do, until Jesus interrupts our grief. He always
finds a way to come, change us, in one way or another.

49

Love multiplies its words without ever repeating.

How could it? That would be like two babies or trees,
exactly the same. That would be like a predictable response,
a graph which accurately plots human interactions.

Take my wife! She's new every time she comes down the steps;
with the dog, without the dog, new sewing or a painting,
her piano lesson. And who knows what's up at the grocers!

Love comes, happy as summer leaves. The reign
of God, in breezes, pattering, just so He can get
a rise out of every midrib, the larger shift

and bob of the branches as well. Grass is slower,
but it too, like an old friend, pushes back. It is Jesus
who reveals Himself in this process. He reaches, answers

with a self He creates. The play is what makes us whole,
the coax and finish determine the us we choose
to reveal. And we're not alone. There are many strangers

around us, more gifts than we would have thought possible.
That fact reveals itself immediately: in syntax—
those holy ropes we skip, playing the next game.

Ask for more. Ask better, and although you
are very far from perfection, ask Me for it
unceasingly in order to bring you nearer to Me.

If enough sun comes in, the windows will open.
Frost steams off the motor scooter tarp out back.
Hope lives! He just walked past on the morning alley!

So what if he didn't stop. Maybe he was on
an errand. The world is bigger than you and me.
Maybe He was off to create a county in Ireland;

maybe He was up for some clogging. Don't worry, we'll all
have crucifixes bouncing around our sweaty necks.
I'll make seven new friends, learn a local saying or two.

All may yet be well, me walking back to my B&B:
though some bodach on the porch might choose to continue the fray.
(My wife's feet will stick out still from the end of the bed.)

I'll think about changing my name to Ronan O'Flaherty.
I mean, it couldn't hurt, two mice peeking out
from one hole. I'd still have to put my knee britches on.

But awash with good will, I'll set out to find a job
in the morning, medals of my patron saints in my pocket.
I'll work next to some spailpin, him jabbering half the day.

Any suffering that you offer Me with love eases
My sufferings, You know that I saw everything
in advance, right to the end of the world.

Our pain is never so. It belongs to others.
We try to hide our gestures, give what passes;
try to let that fade into God's oriental dance.

Great songs deliver both, don't they? They carry
a torch for what lasts, even while delivering what doesn't,
maybe because it's restraint, longing, which define us.

Made human, we find we must embody our art,
that part of us we have to withhold. It's what happens
when we forget ourselves and learn, again,

the cost of belonging—to God's Opened Heart, each painful
wound widening to include everyone we will ever
meet. We move with Jesus on His cross. Rocks roll

to a stop. Each nail, driven into that flesh makes
its future sense, not ours to know. We've long
been a part of this, not predestined, but desired,

like a drop of love which falls on us from His twisted,
draining face—abject art before its time.
God never works outside of the moment we're in!

November 9—*at Mass.*
  I was watching someone come in.

Couldn't you sacrifice your eyes for Me?

We miss the other church, where everything alive
moves in the wind. The back of a centipede, the peddling
blades of leaves. Even the rocks can feel it, a place

so full of life that it gathers in the silence that roseates
windows; the flush of angelic cheeks. Love reins
Itself in, because the King sets the tone in this place.

We run for days here and no one hides, shiny
pennies every way we turn. This is the Holy
Eucharist, heaven Itself, the God who won't spurn.

We reach, then settle, in the creak of our shiny pews.
Who can take us from here, eternity's anteroom.
Jesus, our maker and molder, He's written it down.

(You can hear the scratching of His pen, Him shake out the paper
to facilitate its drying.) "Come, be with Me now.
Dip into the well—and more, its sky, your refuge.

The rest will come to you as It always has.
I offer the rose, the Bread-born, your heavenly end."
And the child in us, though antsy, chooses again to wait.

Your thoughts are short, but at least prolong your
desires so that you can reach a higher plane—
the new heights where the Spirit is waiting
for you to help you to climb even higher.

We hope we can be that reach, the heart that endures
the man. We hope our arc will help to fashion us
a sky big enough to open. But these sordid thoughts,

they straggle, like men who hardly know themselves.
They contend, set up their little bibs on Malibu beach,
dissolve before they can finish their line in the sand.

We want to be players, dammit. We want some land,
to invent a better beer. We want to have friends
like we see on tv commercials. There's no end to this.

We are unredeemable. I mean, look at us.
Nureyev does not attend us in the bathroom. Our actions
are soiled the moment we touch them. And You want me to climb

higher. I suppose I could at least be calm,
rappel as the situation demands, find a suitable station;
the unclicking, necessary to come to my place on the ground.

We can blink after a while. Don't know if that will help.
We would like everything He has for us. But this death
comes first. For Francis, Augustine, it never left.

*Go over my favors and see if your life will
be long enough to thank me for them.*

Thank You for the bees, those little protagonists;
they do not splay the truth to make the sun shine.
They don't remake the world afresh, into their own image.

If they have a beef, it is with a flower. The blue
is their calculus. Each day, they can't believe it when they
wake up, surrounded by so many friends,

something to do each minute! Birds and grasshoppers
help write the script. Each day is a wind; the talk
in the hive only adds to the scope of heaven's adventure.

Colors kill them: the glorious throats of flowers.
Who could've foreseen that, the fuzz in collecting?
The earth is a large gift! It sways right in front

of them. This is their theology of the body. Jesus speaks
in clouds, in tears which test their wings! When they die
they know they will stay here forever; their bellies will tilt

the universe. That given world will bring first honey.
(Eden, for them, was not so long ago.)
Freshened, it'll be time to open that easy door.

Don't talk out of yourself, but out of Me.

It always starts from somewhere else, doesn't it:
a slight wind or some rain in a downspout, that larger thing
that needs to be heard or felt—and you're in your place.

The trick is to stay there; not easy, especially when
you've got so much to say, all your mad little soldiers,
how you would crash one over the other as a kid.

But the local is not the larger picture, nor is it,
perhaps, purely here, in the end: it's the authentic face
you're allowed to wear, the will and skin of God.

When the late spring comes, in May, early June, you take
the life that has started, hurry outside to the green
which has moved past the cozening up stage. You celebrate.

The season speaks the Holy Spirit—all you have
to do is walk. The fullish-green leaves swim
in the trees above the parking lot. They sound like bears:

that choreographed motion, many limbs, growling out
a windy joy. That's what we say: Jesus—
a finer impetuosity—help us to catch Your salmon.

*My little girl, do you know when you speak like
Me? . . . When you touch hearts . . . When you
remain humble without seeking to shine."*

So many people do this! Those who light
the street lamps at night or take care of the bodies after people
die. The cobbler who closes his door, crawls into

his bed alone. Beatrix Potter's already
written that Christmas story: "The Tailor of Glouchester,"
though the sun begins to rise higher—like the molt

from a casting ladle here in Weirton, where dogs
will want out, expect biscuits. Every spear of grass
tingles in what's bigger (a million little soldiers saluting

each breeze). An old man on our street is being sung as well,
stretching in his slippers; he takes each day as his last.
He knows that Jesus only comes because He's here.

The rest of our invented town knows this as well,
and soon too many Fords are starting up
and down the street. That's why God invented Gaudi.

Don't ask for a conclusion. It was here before we started.
Praise like sun in rain: you give your hand
and your whole body gets wet. You have to change clothes.

This work can save a sinner as can any effort to overcome yourself. Let this encourage you.

—*for TH*

Someone's finger moves, a flower continues to open.
Who knows what is happening here? You open a door
for someone and a war stops, two hundred years

ago. You don't have to visit, you've already been there.
Who knows how many friends you have, and where?
We could be in Glasgow even now, sipping scotch,

or signing the Magna Carta. More than likely, though,
you'd be tossing peat into the fire, finding your knees
when the tv age finally comes. The grain in the floor

owns us. It's where we find ourselves at the end
of each working day: with calyx or stem, anything
rough-hewn, hearty. This is the encouragement our betters

offer. St. Francis on his knees, right down there with you:
the whole flower or an oven mitt lifting the steaming kettle.
Our yeses are modest, but such is heaven's charm.

One bird flies with the many, and so the sound
of his wing escapes him. In a way, that's too bad: his breathing
and muscle against the bluffs and push of the wind.

Begin, begin right from this very moment.
Tighten the bonds of union. Ask the immaculate
one for this grace. Her heart never left me.

She, without sin, hesitated. It's enough to make you laugh.
(Just when you thought the greatest could be no smaller!)
She was just a human, hanging onto the grace of God.

Jesus and His mother, kindly picking up behind.
Nature and grace. Burns and Allen. Who could write
across that sky? No matter. In heaven claves clack,

music runs high. We each are given a fitting
instrument. The air blows through us—His song dances
with ours. We are finger holes, made to do this damage.

We want union; we want to shake the past.
Take us from here—to here. We want to be
Your quiet. (We could flap a collection of colorful flags,

exhume our thoughtful dead. But the corpses won't dance.)
Mother, we need more than we can ever say.
Don't leave us to ourselves. We will surely be lost. Finish

what you and He have started. Your hand would gently
touch my shoulder; your smile would bring me again
to that stutter—the only heartening that ever matters.

*Be fully aware of Me in those around you, and,
without stopping to contemplate Me, serve Me in
them. Later on you will be glad of this.*

—for MAS

This is what it means to get lost in the crowd.
Your face could be anybody's, your rousing good humor
could set a tone you could, anonymously, follow.

The King lives here, leans against every lamppost.
You don't have to go home because you don't live there either.
You want to carry on so Love can lay Its head.

It's always the tender, smallest exchange that gets us:
the gesture we have to notice to see. When it comes
on a tv, it catches our throats, delivers God's tears.

This is heaven seeping through the only way
it ever does. This goes on everywhere: in the attention
a colleague gives to a student's computer message.

Her heart is so big, she'd give it away to a school!
You can ride that same bus; a dime in the slot and you're not
in your office, but skipping down a street. On some silly errand,

maybe with a chance to free up your burdened wife.
She's driven, works much harder than anyone should.
And you, you can use all the deaths that you can get!

*These are My virtues and they are so powerful
that even the worldly admire them. But
you must let yourself be adorned. You must
turn your will to your highest good.*

That'll be the day we own the sky, unrationed;
everyone will speak with the same words. I will know
you as I do now, but face to face. Our adornment

will be each other, like the college friend who once told
me about his life. (That seemed to admit me!) He raged
at the food pantry priest who checked the quality

of his family's curtains. (It always feels like kneeling
down, hearing someone talk about his life.)
Our Lady weeps—still heaven, and so I'll learn

what birds feel like living on air. We seek
that cross in the people we meet each day: the King's robe;
we want some evidence of what has happened here!

If I could touch the hem of His garment, the world
would become clear. Until then, our friendships will have
to do—provide us with the occasional glimpse of heaven.

If you have time, friend, pull up at our noisy table.
We'll buy some wine for the occasion. These days fly by
so quickly, like horses—and then everybody will be gone!

Endnotes

1. I actually had a dream which seemed to tell me to be more like a middling pick-up basketball player I know by the name of Ed Ross. Ed has long made doing his duty a focus in his life.
2. Shelly found a great friend in Byron, but when Percy learned that his new pal's family had a crest (Shelley's didn't), he felt, I have to say it, crestfallen.
3. The virtuous pagans belong to Dante, as does their admittance.
4. This form of the ghazal, or ghazal look-alike, was lifted from Bly who has the box elder tree in one of his poems. He is from Minnesota.

www.ingramcontent.com/pod-product-compliance
Lightning Source LLC
Chambersburg PA
CBHW060425050426
42449CB00009B/2146